D1613505

The Great Big Book of
DINOSAURS

Published in 1993 by Wishing Well Books,
an imprint of Joshua Morris Publishing, Inc.,
221 Danbury Road, Wilton, CT 06897.
This edition has been published by
arrangement with Gareth Stevens, Inc.
ISBN: 0-88705-697-0
Manufactured in China
10 9 8 7 6 5 4 3 2 1

KYORYUTACHI (DINOSAURS)
by Mitsuhiro Kurokawa
Copyright © 1987 by Mitsuhiro Kurokawa.
American translation rights arranged with
Koguma Publishing Co., Ltd.
through Japan Foreign-Rights Centre.

English translation and format © 1989 by Gareth Stevens, Inc.
Additional text and illustrations © 1989 by Gareth Stevens, Inc.

Supervising paleontologist: Dr. Ikuo Obata, Director,
Geological Institute, National Science Museum of Japan
Consulting paleontologist (U.S.): Diane Gabriel,
Milwaukee Public Musem
Designer: Geri Strigenz
Editors (U.S.): Pat Walsh, Kelli Peduzzi, and Scott Enk
Additional end matter: Daniel Helminak

The Great Big Book of
DINOSAURS

Mitsuhiro Kurokawa

WISHING WELL BOOKS

Introduction

Millions of years before the first human beings walked the Earth, our planet was home to dinosaurs and other prehistoric animals.

In some ways, these incredible animals were much like animals of today. Some had sharp teeth and horns, while others looked quite gentle. Some were as small as a present-day chicken, but others were bigger than a house. Some prehistoric insects looked much like insects we see all around us — only much bigger.

Of course, most of these animals no longer exist. We know about them only because people continue to find their remains, about 65 million years after the last dinosaur died.

Studying the remains of these animals has caused us to change some of the ideas we have had about pre-historic life. And our learning continues. Who knows? Maybe you will one day learn something we never knew before about this fascinating period in the history of our Earth!

Table of Contents

The sea swells with early life

Millions of years ago, somewhere in the deep, dark murk of the sea, prehistoric creatures called protozoans slowly grew and took shape. Protozoan means "first animal." In the beginning, these first animals were one-celled and smaller than a grain of sand. They ate plants even tinier than themselves. Gradually, the first underwater animals became more complex and had many cells. This did not happen all at once, but over millions and millions of years.

Some of these many-celled animals evolved into other creatures. Evolved means to change into a more highly organized form. Some many-celled animals evolved into jellyfish. Another group evolved into sea urchins and starfish. Over time, colorful corals and sea anemones evolved. These early underwater animals ate plants and smaller animals.

The animals came in fantastic shapes and colors. Translucent jellyfish floated like ghosts in the blue water. Brilliant white coral grew into sculptural forms. Sand-colored starfish and spiky sea urchins searched for food along the bottom. All the creatures moved with the gentle waving of the sea.

DID YOU KNOW?
Coral is a many-celled animal that often joins with other corals to form colorful coral reefs.
Crinoids are also called sea lilies. Their bodies formed limestone beds at prehistoric sea bottoms.
Graptolithina were early relatives of today's jellyfish that had many small floats around one large one.
Jellyfish, still existing today, catch prey with tentacles and move by shooting water from their bodies.
Michelinoceras had its feet in front of its eyes and could swim as well as crawl on the sea bottom.
Sea pens still exist today. They are distant relatives of sea anemones and corals.
Sea scorpions had five pairs of legs, including one pair with paddles. They used the paddles to crush prey.
Snails can move with one foot and live in tightly coiled shells where they can hide for protection.
Sponges, which still live all over the world, attach themselves to rocks or sandy sea bottoms.
Spriggina were worms with horseshoe-shaped heads that lived in mud or sand on the seabed.
Starfish still seek food with their arms at the bottom of the sea. They can lie in one place for hours.

PRE-CAMBRIAN TIME

LOWER PALEOZOIC ERA
Cambrian Period ► Ordovician Period ► Silurian Period

Unlike other prehistoric animals, fish continued to evolve. They developed bones, nerves, and brains. They could steer themselves rather than just drift in the water. They ate each other. It was a ferocious world to live in. The first sharklike fish terrorized weaker fish. Sneaky fish hid in weeds until an unsuspecting fish came along. One chomp and the startled victim was devoured.

One kind of fish had armorlike skin on its head, upper body, and fins, which enemy fish could not penetrate. Small, swift fish could flee an enemy. Slow but strong fish could fight back. When danger neared, some fish hid in underwater caves or camouflaged themselves in the sand, lying motionless on the bottom of the sea.

The sea was much shallower than it is now, and the water was warm. The climate was subtropical. This means it was hot, with parched, dry seasons and steamy, rainy seasons. During the rainy season violent thunderstorms roiled the sea. Towering waves crashed onto the beach, carrying unlucky creatures with them, creatures that died because they could not breathe through their gills when they were out of water.

During the dry seasons, the shallowest parts of the sea evaporated. Some fish swam to the deepest water they could find, while other fish adapted to this temporary predicament. They developed special air bladders which enabled them to breathe out of water like we do with our lungs. Fish continued to evolve in response to changes in their environment.

DID YOU KNOW?
Cladoselache was an ancestor of today's sharks. Its sleek body and large tail helped it swim quickly.
Coelacanths were thought to be extinct for many years, until one was caught near South Africa in 1938.
Dinichthys has a name that means "terrible fish." It was not a good swimmer, but it had strong jaws.
Trilobites were early relatives of today's crabs and spiders. There were more than 2,500 kinds.

LOWER PALEOZOIC ERA ► UPPER PALEOZOIC ERA
Silurian Period ► Devonian Period ► Carboniferous Period

9

Out of the water onto the land

One of the most dramatic moments in the evolution of animals happened during a dry spell, when the first fish had to drag itself out of ebbing water and onto land in search of deeper water. Pulling itself along with sturdy fins, it breathed through its air bladder and desperately inched across swampy land. When it finally found a pool, it dove in with relief and began breathing through its gills again.

Only those fish that could adapt to conditions on land survived until they reached deeper water. The animals with the sturdiest limbs and most efficient air bladders thrived and passed on these traits to their offspring.

We call these adaptable fish amphibians. Amphibians are able to live on both land and water. As amphibians evolved, they came onto the land by choice. But they had to go back into the water often to keep their skin from drying out, which would have suffocated them. They could live a double life — on land and in water — because they alternated breathing through their lungs, gills, and skin.

DID YOU KNOW?
Cacops had armored plates on its back that kept it from bending but protected it from other animals.
Cotylosaurus, like other early reptiles, evolved from prehistoric amphibians but looked much like a lizard.
Dimetrodon had a large "sail" on its back that it might have used to keep warm or cool, as it needed.
Diplocaulus had a head shaped like a crescent or a triangle. Its gills were under its giant head.
Edaphosaurus, like Dimetrodon, had a large "sail" to regulate body temperature. It probably ate plants.
Eusthenopteron, a relative of the coelacanth, was one of the first fish to crawl onto land and breathe air.
Gerrothorax had a flattened head and a brightly colored mouth that it used to attract prey.
Ichthyostega was the first known amphibian. It evolved from fish and had both legs and fins.
Mastodonsaurus was 12 to 15 feet (3½ to 4½ m) long, the largest amphibian ever.
Meganeura looked like a giant dragonfly with a wingspan of about 30 inches (76 cm).
Proganochelys was a primitive turtle, with sharp spines on its head and tail and sharp scales on its legs.
Seymouria, a reptile that was nearly an amphibian, was a link between reptiles and amphibians.
Stenodictia was one of the first insects with wings. Its wings grew out of flaps on the bodies of its ancestors.

UPPER PALEOZOIC ERA
Carboniferous Period ► Permian Period

11

The birth of reptiles

Reptiles evolved from amphibians. They are considered the first true land animals because they didn't need to go back into water to survive. Their skin and eggs did not dry out on land. Reptiles could eat, live, and reproduce under a great variety of conditions, so they thrived.

Some reptiles had tall fins, or sails, on their backs to help regulate their body temperatures. Some had crests on their heads that could even regulate their brain temperatures! Some developed tiny front legs that they used like hands to grab plants. Others had sharp teeth and powerful jaws that helped them tear meat. Some reptiles were able to walk on two legs.

As reptiles got bigger and bigger, they evolved into dinosaurs.

DID YOU KNOW?
Coelophysis, one of the first dinosaurs, was only about 6 feet (2 m) long. It was fast and graceful.
Cynognathus, a reptile, was like mammals in many ways. It had hair and might have nursed its young.
Dicynodon lived in both the time before the dinosaurs and the early days of the dinosaurs.
Dilophosaurus had a pair of crests on its head that might have controlled the temperature of its brain.
Euparkeria, one of the first archosaurs, could run on its hind legs, using its tail for balance.
Fabrosaurus did not leave many traces of itself for scientists. We know it mainly from a part of its jawbone.
Heterodontosaurus ("different-toothed reptile") had both nipping and pointed teeth for eating plants.
Lesothosaurus was one of the first plant-eating dinosaurs. Its teeth were especially suited for its diet.
Longisquama had long scales on its back. It may have been an ancestor of later gliding or flying animals.
Lufengosaurus is named after the Chinese city of Lufeng, in Yunan Province, where its remains were found.
Lystrosaurus was a pre-dinosaur era reptile. It has been found in Antarctica and places close to the South Pole.
Machaeroprosopus, first found in the Painted Desert in northern Arizona, was an ancestor of the crocodile.
Moschops was a bulky, mammal-like plant-eater that lived in what is now South Africa.
Ornithosuchus was a fast-moving meat-eater with armor on its back. Remains have been found in Scotland.
Plateosaurus, the largest reptile of its time, usually walked on its hind legs but could walk on all four legs.
Scelidosaurus was the first dinosaur with armored plates on its body. Its name means "ribbed reptile."
Staurikosaurus was small for a meat-eater at 6 feet (2 m) in length, but it had strong jaws and teeth.
Syntarsus, found in places as far apart as North America and Africa, was a fast-running dinosaur.
Teratosaurus, the first large flesh-eating dinosaur, was 50 feet (15 m) long and weighed over half a ton.

UPPER PALEOZOIC ERA ► MESOZOIC ERA
Permian Period ► Triassic Period

Dinosaurs rule the Earth

Dinosaurs were extraordinary creatures. Some were bigger than a house; others, smaller than a chicken. Scales covered thick hides. Ridges, horns, and bumps protruded from heads and backs. Long tails swung from side to side, helping the creatures balance as they walked. Claws and teeth looked ferocious.

Some animals began to develop feathers. Paleontologists (scientists who study prehistoric times) think the feathers kept animals warm and were useful when an animal swooped from tree to tree or parachuted to the ground or leaped high into the air to catch prey.

Dinosaurs could roam the Earth because when they reigned, all the continents were one huge land mass.

The air the dinosaurs breathed was hot and humid. Great jungles thrived. There was so much to eat that dinosaurs roamed in great herds, eating their way across the green world. They sheltered their young in the center of the herd. Plant-eaters, called herbivores, led a contented life but for one problem — meat-eaters!

DID YOU KNOW?
Alocodon, "wing-tooth," was mistaken for Fabrosaurus. It was only about 3 feet (1 m) long.
Antrodemus (Allosaurus), although large, could run quickly to capture prey.
Archeopteryx is considered to be the first bird, but it could not fly — it only glided from tree to tree.
Ceratosaurus, or "horned reptile," may have hunted its prey in groups, much as wolves do.
Coelurus had three-fingered "hands." It was large, but light, so it could jump to catch even flying prey.
Dimorphodon was a flying reptile whose skull was large and open. It had large hind legs with big claws.
Elaphrosaurus lived in eastern Africa. What we know about it we learned only from a skeleton without a skull.
Kentrosaurus, from near Lake Tanganyika, in Africa, had six pairs of spines running down its back and tail.
Metriacanthosaurus, long mistaken for Megalosaurus, had large, sharp spines on its back.
Ornitholestes was small but swift. Its name means "bird-robber," but it probably preferred eating lizards.
Rhamphorhynchus was only about as big as a modern robin. It flew close to the water, scooping up fish.
Saltopus was small, only about 2 feet (60 cm) long as an adult. A meat-eater, it left birdlike tracks.
Segisaurus, known only through a few skeletal remains, was like a larger version of Compsognathus.
Toujiangosaurus had a spiky tail and 15 tinlike plates along its back for heat control or protection.

MESOZOIC ERA
Triassic Period

The roar of the carnivorous, or meat-eating, dinosaurs sent other animals scurrying in fear. Carnivores had the speed and strength to catch even the largest herbivores. The carnivores had slashing claws and ripping teeth especially suited for eating flesh.

But many dinosaurs had ways to protect themselves. Some developed armored hides and hard skin. Their bellies were soft and vulnerable but only the strongest foes could have pushed them over to gash them. One armored dinosaur was so well protected that predators would often give up trying to bring it down. Some dinosaurs with spiked tails could use them to club their predators.

Other herbivores protected themselves from predators with sharp spines on their backs. Even the hungriest predator did not want a meal that was too painful to dine on comfortably!

Though they were easy prey, the herbivores survived because there were more of them than the carnivores could eat.

DID YOU KNOW?
Apatosaurus (Brontosaurus), the big fellow, ate up to 1,000 pounds (450 kg) of food a day.
Camarasaurus had a skull like that of Apatosaurus, so museums mistakenly put it on Apatosaurus skeletons!
Compsognathus, the smallest dinosaur, was about the size of a chicken and preyed on small lizards.
Diplodocus had the longest body of all dinosaurs but it was light. It had peglike teeth for chewing plants.
Dryosaurus, with long legs, was about 10 to 12 feet (3 to 3.6 m) long but ran quickly and gracefully.
Megalosaurus, the second dinosaur to be discovered, had a heavy skeleton and sharp claws.
Pterodactylus, only the size of a pigeon, had a furry body and limbs and light, hollow bones to help it fly.
Sordes, which was not a dinosaur but a flying reptile, had delicate bones and few teeth. It lived near water.
Stegosaurus was the largest dinosaur with plates on its back. These may have helped control its temperature.
Yangchuanosaurus, a ferocious meat-eater found in what is now China, had a supple neck and tail.

MESOZOIC ERA
Triassic Period ► Jurassic Period

The world of the dinosaurs changes

Over millions of years, the Earth's land mass broke into the continents we know today. Volcanoes erupted. Hot lava flowed over dinosaurs unfortunate enough to be caught in its path. The lava fossilized the dinosaurs' bodies. The Earth's landscape was permanently changed.

The climate changed, too. Temperature, rainfall, and plant cycles followed patterns, forming seasons. A moderate climate allowed new vegetation to grow. Hardwood trees grew into dense forests. Flowering plants spread pale blossoms over the landscape.

Dinosaurs still evolved millions of years after their first appearance. Those weighing 60 tons had to spend the day eating in order to fuel their bodies. They could eat 1,000 pounds (450 kg) of plants a day. In four months, they ate their body weight in food.

All dinosaurs hatched from eggs that were anywhere from the size of a chicken egg to the size of a melon. Dinosaurs grew up differently depending on whether they lived in herds or by themselves. A dinosaur born into a herd had parents that cared for it until it could feed and defend itself. One kind of dinosaur raised its young in nurserylike nests! Instinct told other kinds of dinosaurs how to feed and defend themselves.

DID YOU KNOW?
Brachiosaurus, at about 80 tons, had front legs longer than its hind legs and nostrils on the top of its head.
Camptosaurus had short front legs, but scientists think its thick "fingers" mean it often walked on all four legs.
Deinonychus, small but fierce, had three toes — with one more like a claw — and probably hunted in packs.
Dracopelta lived in what is now Portugal. It might be the earliest armored dinosaur.
Mamenchisaurus had a neck as long as its body and tail combined. It was the biggest dinosaur living in Asia.
Minmi was the first armored dinosaur discovered in the Southern Hemisphere. It lived in what is now Australia.
Rhamphorhynchus, a flying reptile that ate fish, had leathery wings and a long tail useful as a rudder.
Tenontosaurus was a fast, long-tailed runner from what is now Montana. Its name means "sinewy reptile."
Ultrasaurus, the biggest of them all, probably weighed 100 tons and was as tall as a five-story building.

MESOZOIC ERA
Jurassic Period ► Cretaceous Period

19

The voice of the dinosaur

The dinosaurs lived in a world of echoing sound. Volcanoes rumbled, rain beat down, waterfalls crashed on the rocks, wind swept through branches, lightning struck and set trees to a crackling blaze. Dinosaur feet thudded on hard ground. They thrashed through the dense undergrowth, chewing and chomping on leafy mouthfuls.

Dinosaurs had voices. They trumpeted the danger alarm when a predator was near or cried in agony when attacked. They sang their mysterious mating songs and communicated with their young with familiar sounds. Dinosaurs groaned, grunted, growled, and grumbled. Dinosaurs sniffed, snorted, screeched, and screamed.

Dinosaurs plunged into water to escape their hunters. Some dinosaurs relaxed in water. Since their nostrils were on the tops of their heads, they could submerge most of their bulky bodies. All that could be heard was contented breathing.

DID YOU KNOW?
Corythosaurus, "helmeted reptile," is one of the best known duck-billed dinosaurs. It lived near marshes.
Hadrosaurus, a duckbill, was the first dinosaur to leave a nearly complete skeleton. It was discovered in 1858.
Hypsilophodon, with rows of bony lumps on its back, might have used its long toes and fingers to climb trees.
Iguanodon had spikelike thumbs that scientists thought were horns until they found 30 complete skeletons in 1878.
Lambeosaurus, found in Alberta, Canada, had a good sense of smell and a loud bellow!
Maiasaura, the smallest duckbill, had a flat tail for swimming. Parents raised the young in "nurseries."
Ouranosaurus was like Iguanodon in many ways, but it had a "sail" down its back.
Parasaurolophus had a crest extending 4 feet (1.5 m) from the back of its head. This may have helped it smell.
Polacanthus, about 12 to 15 feet (3.6 to 4.6 m) long, had both spikes and a hard "shield" over its hips.
Protoceratops had a hard, well-developed "frill" behind its head. Fossils of its eggs and young are numerous.
Psittacosaurus had a hard, parrotlike beak. It was an early ancestor of horned dinosaurs like Triceratops.
Saurolophus had a large, pointed crest of bone on its head. It may have used this to attract mates or repel rivals.
Shantungosaurus was the largest duck-billed dinosaur. It was about 40 feet (12 m) long and lived in China.
Tsintaosaurus had a large spike on top of its head, but the spike was weak, so it was not useful for fighting.

MESOZOIC ERA
Cretaceous Period

Fighters and their prey

Most of the meat-eating dinosaurs were killers. These predators were the strongest, most ferocious animals that ever lived. Their dagger-sharp teeth, powerful jaws, and vicious claws were useful for killing prey. Flying carnivores could swoop down on other animals, catching them in their mouths or claws.

Some dinosaurs could run very fast from a predator. But they would soon get tired and have to find a good hiding place before another attacker came along. Other dinosaurs, like Triceratops, could defend themselves with long, sharp horns and thick plates on their bodies. These dinosaurs were smaller and gentler than their ferocious killers. But if threatened by a predator, they would fight to the death.

Dinosaurs did not just fight to kill food or defend their families. Meat-eating dinosaurs of the same species often fought each other to see who was stronger. These dinosaurs had skulls with thick bones which protected their brains during the fight. The fighters would knock their heads together as hard as they could. Crack! If one dinosaur was killed, or gave up the fight, his opponent became the leader of the herd.

DID YOU KNOW?
Albertosaurus, from Canada, was a fearsome carnivore, smaller than Tyrannosaurus but probably faster.
Alioramus, one of the last dinosaurs to live in Asia, had a bump between its eyes and nose.
Edmontosaurus, a herd animal, moved in herds and ate leaves from cypress and other swamp trees.
Monoclonius, like Triceratops and other horned dinosaurs, resembled today's rhinoceros in many ways.
Nodosaurus had a tanklike cover of armored plates, but unlike some armored dinosaurs, it had no tail spikes.
Parksosaurus had large eyes in a small head, a horny beak for digging roots, and long toes.
Quetzalcoatlus is the largest known flying animal that ever lived. It had a wingspan of 39 feet (12 m).
Stenonychosaurus, from North America, grabbed with its long arms. We still aren't sure how to classify it.
Styracosaurus had a frill with six sharp spikes that it probably used to frighten enemies, not fight them.
Tarbosaurus is a close relative of Tyrannosaurus that lived in Mongolia. Its name means "fearsome lizard."

MESOZOIC ERA
Cretaceous Period

Some meat-eating dinosaurs were not killers. They were scavengers. Scavengers eat leftovers from another animal's kill. Tyrannosaurus, the largest meat-eater and probably a scavenger, could gulp down enormous chunks of food. It didn't even have to chew them!

Flying scavengers sought a fresh kill from the air. They swooped down, snatched meat from the killer, and quickly flew to safety to eat their food.

Small carnivores found nests full of eggs, ate them, and skulked away before a parent returned. The ancestors of today's sea turtles would swim near schools of small fish and gobble a few before swimming away to their next meal.

Over millions of years, the battles between fighters and their prey continued. Some kinds of dinosaurs dominated others by winning all their fights, while other kinds died out. But it must have seemed that dinosaurs would always rule the world.

The dinosaurs ruled Earth for 140 million years. This may seem like a long time compared to the age of Earth itself, which is about five billion years old! From the dinosaurs' point of view, the world was changing so gradually that it didn't seem very different from day to day. But in fact, the world was about to change very drastically for the dinosaurs.

DID YOU KNOW?
Dsungaripterus, from what is now China, liked lakes and ate fish. It had a wingspan of up to 9 feet (3 m).
Euoplocephalus had armor, large nostrils, and a horny beak. Some scientists think its tail was used as a club.
Oviraptor, "egg thief," was about as big as a turkey. Fossilized eggs have been found with its skeleton.
Pachycephalosaurus had a bony dome on its head. Battling males probably used this as a battering ram.
Spinosaurus had a 6-foot (1.8-m) "sail" on its back that probably regulated its body temperature like a radiator.
Struthiomimus, a herd animal, could have run as fast as today's ostrich — 50 miles (80 km) an hour.
Torosaurus had a skull 8 feet (2.5 m) long. It was one of the last dinosaurs.
Triceratops had a heavily horned and armored head, which may have helped it outlive other dinosaurs.
Tyrannosaurus, the largest carnivore, could dislocate its jaws and gulp down food as big as a man in one bite.

MESOZOIC ERA
Cretaceous Period

25

The dinosaurs vanish mysteriously

The last dinosaur died 65 million years ago. Scientists still do not know why they disappeared. Some think a huge meteorite struck the Earth, gouging out a crater and filling the air with choking dust. The dust blocked out all the sunlight, killing the plants that the dinosaurs fed on. The world may have been frozen in a deep winter for many years. The dinosaurs would have been unable to adapt to the sudden change in temperature and the loss of their food supply. They all died, but smaller animals may have been able to live off tree bark, frozen seeds, or the bodies of the dead animals. They survived.

After millions of years of evolution, dinosaurs are extinct. That means they are no longer around and they have no living descendants. But many kinds of fish, birds, reptiles, and insects from the age of dinosaurs did survive whatever killed off the dinosaurs. Some, like the coelacanth, turtle, cockroach, and opossum, are still here today.

We should learn a lesson from what happened to the dinosaurs. Scientists have warned us that as we pollute our world, we are destroying the ozone layer of our atmosphere. Without this ozone shield, the Sun would burn us and Earth would become a desert that could not sustain human and most animal life. We must be careful with the ways we use air, water, land, fuel, and food so that present life on the planet does not follow the dinosaurs into extinction!

DID YOU KNOW?

Archelon, at about three tons, was more than twice as big as a modern sea turtle but probably had similar habits.

Pteranodon had a crest at the back of its head, doubling the length of its skull but perhaps aiding it in flight.

MESOZOIC ERA
Cretaceous Period

To read more about the days of the dinosaurs

The books listed below will tell you more about dinosaurs and their world. If you do not find these books at your local library or bookstore, ask someone there to order them for you.

About Dinosaurs. Morris (Penguin)
The Age of Dinosaurs! Parker (Gareth Stevens)
All New Dinosaurs and Their Friends from the Great Recent Discoveries. Long & Wells (Bellerophon)
Amazing Facts About Prehistoric Animals. Craig (Doubleday)
Amazing World of Dinosaurs. Granger (Troll)
Archaeopteryx. Oliver (Rourke)
Brontosaurus Moves In. Austin (Pocket Books)
Brontosaurus, the Thunder Lizard. Halstead (Western)
Did Comets Kill the Dinosaurs? Asimov (Gareth Stevens)
Digging Up Dinosaurs. Aliki (Harper & Row)
Dinosaur Encyclopedia. Benton (Simon & Schuster)
Dinosaurs. Jackson (National Geographic Society)
Dinosaurs and Other Archosaurs. Zallinger (Random House)
Dinosaurs and Other Prehistoric Animals. Geis (Platt & Munk)
Dinosaurs and Their World. Pringle (Harcourt Brace Jovanovich)
Dinosaurs and Their Young. Freedman (Holiday House)
Dinosaurs Are Different. Aliki (Cromwell)
Dinosaur Time. Parish (Starstream Products)
Dinosaur World. Lambert (Franklin Watts)
Doctor Who and the Dinosaur Invasion. Hulke (Pinnacle)
Fossils Tell of Long Ago. Aliki (Harper & Row)
Giant Dinosaurs. Rowe (Scholastic Book Service)
How Did We Find Out about Dinosaurs? Asimov (Avon)
How to Draw Dinosaurs. LaPlaca (Troll)
The Last Days of the Dinosaurs. Gabriele (Penny Lane)
The New Dinosaur Library series (Gareth Stevens)
    The First Dinosaurs. Burton/Dixon
    Hunting the Dinosaurs and Other Prehistoric Animals. Burton/Dixon
    The Jurassic Dinosaurs. Burton/Dixon
    The Last Dinosaurs. Burton/Dixon
Pteranodon. Wilson (Rourke)
Sea Monsters: Ancient Reptiles that Ruled the Sea. Eldridge (Troll)
Stegosaurus. Sheehan (Rourke)
Super Book of Dinosaurs and Prehistoric Animals. Daly (Troll)
Tyrannosaurus Wrecks: A Book of Dinosaur Riddles. Stern (Harper & Row)
Whatever Happened to the Dinosaurs? Jaber (Messner)

To see the world of dinosaurs

Try to plan a visit to one of the museums listed below. They will have exhibits showing dinosaurs in settings that resemble their natural environment as well as other animal and plant species that lived in the prehistoric world.

Academy of Natural Sciences
Philadelphia, Pennsylvania

American Museum of Natural History
New York, New York

Denver Museum of Natural History
Denver, Colorado

Geological Museum
Laramie, Wyoming

Museum of Natural History
Lawrence, Kansas

Museum of the Rockies
Bozeman, Montana

North Carolina Museum of
    Life and Science
Durham, North Carolina

And for more information

The libraries and museums listed below contain exhibits that you can view. They also have education offices that will provide you with additional information about dinosaurs and other prehistoric life. When you write to them, be sure to tell them exactly what you would like to know and include your name, address, and age.

Carnegie Museum of Natural History
Division of Education
4400 Forbes Avenue
Pittsburgh, PA 15213

C.E.U. Prehistoric Museum
451 East 400 North
Price, UT 84501

Dinosaur National Monument
P.O. Box 210
Dinosaur, CO 81610

Dinosaur Provincial Park
Box 60
Patricia, Alberta
Canada   T0J 2K0

Dinosaur State Park
West Street
Rocky Hill, CT 06067

Dinosaur Valleys
362 Main Street
Grand Junction, CO 81501

Field Museum of Natural History
Roosevelt Road at Lake Shore Drive
Chicago, IL 60605

Houston Museum of Natural Sciences
1 Hermann Circle Drive
Houston, TX 77030

Los Angeles County Museum of Natural History
900 Exposition Blvd.
Los Angeles, CA 90007

Milwaukee Public Museum
800 West Wells Street
Milwaukee, WI 53233

National Museum of Natural Sciences
McCloud and Metcalfe
Ottawa, Ontario
Canada   K1P 9Z9

Provincial Museum of Alberta
12845 102nd Avenue
Edmonton, Alberta
Canada   T5N 0M6

Royal Ontario Museum
100 Queen's Park
Toronto, Ontario
Canada   M5S 2C6

Smithsonian Institution
National Museum of Natural History
Office of Education
10th and Constitution Avenue NW
Washington, DC 20560

Tyrell Museum of Paleontology
Box 7500
Drumheller, Alberta
Canada   T0J 0Y0

Utah Museum of Natural History
University of Utah
Salt Lake City, UT 84112

Glossary

Amphibians: cold-blooded animals that are able to live both on land and in water. Amphibians are able to alternate breathing through their lungs, gills, and skin. A frog is an amphibian.

Armored: covered with tough, bony scales.

Camouflage: to hide by taking on the textures and colors of the surrounding area.

Carnivore: an animal that survives by eating the flesh of other animals.

Cell: the smallest part of an organism that is able to function independently.

Crater: an impression in the Earth; a hole shaped by a meteorite hitting the Earth or by an explosion.

Descendant: a living thing that came from an earlier species but may not necessarily resemble it closely.

Environment: everything surrounding and affecting any plant or animal. This includes land, water, and air, for example.

Evolve: to gradually adapt and change over millions of years in response to environmental changes.

Extinction: the death of all members of an animal or plant species. This is usually the result of some sort of change in the land, air, or water around the animal or plant.

Fossils: the remains or traces of animals and plants found in rock formations.

Herbivore: an animal that survives by feeding on plants.

Meteorite: a piece of material from space that passes through the atmosphere and crashes into Earth. Massive destruction can result, depending upon the size of the meteorite.

Ozone: a form of oxygen in the atmosphere that helps to protect all life on Earth from the Sun's harmful radiation.

Paleontologist: a scientist who studies prehistoric life by examining remains of plants and animals.

Predator: an animal that lives by eating other animals; a carnivore.

Prey: an animal that is killed and eaten by another animal.

Protozoans: the most primitive forms of animal life. They are one-celled organisms.

Reptiles: the first true land animals. These animals lay their eggs on land. Their skin consists of horny plates or scales. They are cold-blooded. Lizards, snakes, and crocodiles are reptiles.

Scale: a small, overlapping structure that forms the protective covering of fish and reptiles.

Scavengers: animals that eat leftovers from another animal's kill.

Translucent: capable of allowing light to pass through while at the same time not being clear enough to see through. A stained-glass window is translucent.

Index